P9-CQL-365

WITHDRAWN

Word Bird's

Spring Words

FORT BEND COUNTY LIBRARIES
RICHMOND, TX

Published in the United States of America by The Child's World®, Inc.
PO Box 326
Chanhassen, MN 55317-0326
800-599-READ
www.childsworld.com

Project Manager Mary Berendes
Editor Katherine Stevenson, Ph.D.
Designer Ian Butterworth

Copyright © 2002 by The Child's World®, Inc.
All rights reserved. No part of this book may be
reproduced or utilized in any form or by any means
without written permission from the publisher.

Library of Congress Cataloging-in-Publication Data
Moncure, Jane Belk.
Word Bird's spring words / by Jane Belk Moncure.
p. cm.
Summary: Word Bird puts words about spring in his word house—
mud puddles, shamrocks, seeds, kites, and others.
ISBN 1-56766-896-8 (lib. bdg.)
1. Vocabulary—Juvenile literature. 2. Spring—Juvenile literature.
[1. Vocabulary. 2. Spring.] I. Title.
PE1449 .M53 2001
428.1—dc21
00-010888

Word Bird's

Spring Words

by Jane Belk Moncure

illustrated by Chris McEwan

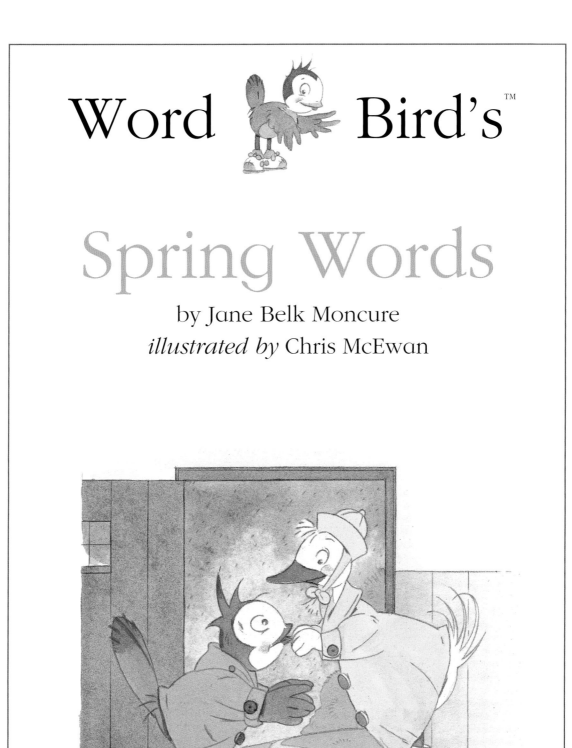

Word Bird made a…

word house.

"I will put spring words
in my house," Word
Bird said.

Word Bird put in
these words:

rain

raincoat

boots

umbrella

mud puddles

tadpoles

frogs

St. Patrick's Day

shamrocks

hoe

seeds

water hose

garden

wind

kites

ball

bat

skates

robins

nest

Easter

Easter basket

daffodils

May baskets

Can you read these spring

rain

tadpoles

raincoat

frogs

boots

St. Patrick's Day

umbrella

hoe

mud puddles

seeds

words with Word Bird?

water hose

skates

garden

robins

wind

nest

kites

Easter

ball

daffodils

bat

May baskets

You can make a spring word house. You can put Word Bird's words in your house and read them, too.

Can you think of other spring words to put in your word house?